Protect Your Child From Sexual Abuse:

A Parent's Guide

A Book to Teach Children
How to Resist Uncomfortable Touch

by Janie Hart-Rossi

This book was adapted from material developed by Janie Hart-Rossi under a grant from Planned Parenthood of Snohomish County.

LC   84-060586

ISBN 943990-06-8   (paper)
ISBN 943990-07-6   (lib. binding)

Parenting Press, Inc.
7750 31st Ave. NE
Seattle, WA 98115

TABLE OF CONTENTS

INTRODUCTION

The goal of this book is to help parents protect their children from sexual abuse. The information and activities presented here are founded upon the fact that children who have been specifically warned about sexual abuse and who have been given a "plan of action" to call upon if a potentially abusive situation occurs, will be less likely to be victimized.

Sexual abuse of children is a scary and horrifying issue; it is difficult for most of us to know how to begin talking to children about this crime. As you read through this book, you will see that there are two main "threads" or concepts emphasized. The first is the belief that teaching sexual abuse prevention to children needs to be, and can be, approached in a calm, matter-of-fact way. Just as we teach our children how to cross the street or how to deal with unfriendly dogs, we can incorporate sexual abuse prevention information into our daily safety teaching.

The second concept, developed in this book, is that parents do need some specific information and methods in order to teach sexual abuse prevention effectively. These methods are based upon giving children the courage to say no to an inappropriate request from an older person.

In a sexually abusive situation, the child is *physically* alone with the offender. He will not try to initiate any abuse unless he is alone with the child. The majority of offenders are very tentative at first. They must be sure the child will cooperate and will not tell anyone else. The child's reaction to this first attempt helps determine whether or not the offender will continue the abuse.

But aware and prepared children are not *emotionally* alone in such a situation. Children who feel good about themselves, and who have had a lot of practice evaluating the actions of others, rejecting those actions which "don't fit" into what they've learned about how people relate to each other, will use their knowledge in a sexually abusive situation. Such children will feel confident about refusing to share their bodies, and they will be more able to reject the offender's insistence that the abuse is a "special secret." These children will tell someone else about what happened.

Most children do not need to be *taught* to feel uncomfortable when they are reluctant to share their bodies. They recognize uncomfortable feelings or warnings that signal, "something is wrong here." However, they do need to be taught that those feelings are real and legitimate, and that communicating those feelings can give them some power in an abusive situation. Reacting assertively, using the phrases and postures taught in *It's MY Body*, protects children by demonstrating to the potential offender: 1) that the child is a person (not an object) who is aware that certain kinds of touch are wrong and that he or she has the right to resist; and 2) that the child will be unlikely to keep any sexually abusive touch secret; the child will tell someone.

This book has been prepared to give parents knowledge and techniques for creating an environment that will make their children more likely to tell someone about an abusive situation.

Parents often feel nervous about the whole subject of sexual abuse. Therefore, the first two chapters give background information to clarify the issues and to provide activities that will help parents become comfortable with matters such as personal space and words for sexual body parts.

The last two chapters provide parents information and activities they can use directly with children. Chapter 3 offers guided reading for the children's book *It's My Body*, by Lory Freeman. Chapter 4 provides a variety of simple ways to build a child's self-esteem, practice a Touching Code, foster decision making and encourage discussion of feelings. These activities will help give children the skills they need to say "No!" to sexual abuse.

A NOTE TO TEACHERS

Although this book was written primarily for parents, teachers will find much of the material useful. Teachers can help children learn skills to resist abusive situations in much the same way as families. You might begin by reading *It's MY Body* to your class, or by adapting some of the activities in Chapter 4. Then you may wish to use the following suggestions to reinforce the concepts presented in this book.

Puppets

It is particularly effective to have the puppets replay situations that have happened between the children in your class, such as pushing, hugging, hitting or holding hands. Guide the children toward relating feelings and touch in these puppet plays: "How do you think George (first puppet) feels inside when Ellie (second puppet) pushes him? What could George say to Ellie?"

A puppet can talk with the class about the times he has noticed the children using the Touching Code or giving "happy" touches. Or, the puppet can tell the class about touching situations that have happened to him.

Pictures and Stories

Use pictures of people touching to tell stories about children using the Touching Code or telling someone about being touched in an uncomfortable way. The children might then be invited to make up stories about the pictures. Encourage them to talk about how the pictured people feel and react to the touch.

Children can be asked to collect magazine pictures of "happy" touches to make a class collage. Collecting the pictures, assembling the collage, hanging it up, and writing a story about it all offer many opportunities for discussing touch, feelings and the Touching Code.

Role Plays

Children can benefit from practicing their Touching Code in a structured situation, such as the following Personal Bubble activity, (page 18).

7

Have everyone stand in a circle. Walk towards an individual child. Have him hold up his hands and say the Touching Code when you get too close. Coach the children not to giggle, but to look at your face and say the Touching Code clearly and sternly.

CHAPTER 1
FACTS YOU NEED TO KNOW ABOUT SEXUAL ABUSE
WHAT IS SEXUAL ABUSE?

Definition

Child sexual abuse occurs when a child is used as an object for the sexual gratification of an adult through manipulation, exploitation, threats, or physical force.

Child sexual abuse also occurs when a child is used as an object of sexual gratification by a minor under 18 years old who is temporarily taking on the parental role (for example, a babysitter).[1]

An example of *manipulation* is: "If you take off your clothes and play with me, I'll let you have two desserts."

An example of *exploitation* is: "This is just my way of showing you I love you."

An example of a *threat* is: "If you don't let me play this game with you, I'll tell your dad what a bad girl you were tonight."

Facts About Sexual Abuse:[2]

One in three girls and one in six boys will have had some kind of sexual contact with an adult by age 18.

The two most common ages at which sexual abuse begins are age eleven and age three. The word *begins* is used here because if there is no intervention from the "outside," an offender will

---

[1] Adapted from: National Center on Child Abuse and Neglect: *Sexual Abuse of Children: Selected Readings* (U.S. Department of Health and Human Services), 1980, p. 1

[2] The statistics on these pages were taken from lectures given during a workshop entitled, "Working With Sexually Abused Children: Discovering the Community Team." October 23-24, 1981. Everett, Washington.

continue sexually abusing the   child, often for years. This is why it is so important that children be   taught to tell someone else immediately if they are touched in an   uncomfortable way by an adult or an older child.

In 75 to 85 percent of sexual abuse cases, the child knows the offender.

One of the "tools" that an offender uses is the child's trust in him. Therefore, most offenders make friends with the child and consciously try to become someone "special" to the child before initiating the abuse.

Sexual abuse offenders and their victims come from all walks of life, all races, and all socio-economic groups.

Myths About Sexual Abuse

Myth: *A sexually abused child somehow encourages or wants the abuse.*

This myth attempts to excuse the behavior of the offender by placing the blame on the victim.

Remember, sexual abuse involves the sexual *use* of a child by someone older, bigger, and more knowledgeable. The offender is *always* responsible for the abuse, *never* the child.

Myth: *Children lie, fantasize, and make up stories about sexual abuse.*

Sexual abuse is NOT something that children make up stories about, lie about, or fantasize about.

Myth: *Sexual abuse cases always involve violence.*

Because the offender wants to keep the abuse a secret, and therefore keep himself protected, physical violence (which would leave clues) is rarely used.

The offender typically uses more subtle forms of power, those of manipulation, exploitation, bribes, and threats.

Prevention Is Possible

A sexual abuse offender counts on the seeming powerlessness of the child. *Sexual abuse prevention involves giving the child some power.*

A sexual abuse offender counts on the child's silence, believing that the child will not tell anyone else about the abuse. *Sexual abuse prevention involves making sure the child will tell someone else about the abuse.*

CHARACTERISTICS OF
SEXUAL ABUSE OFFENDERS

Sexual Abuse Offenders[1]

Sexual abuse offenders are 97% heterosexual males.

"The most extensive study to date reports that the average molester of girl children will molest 62.4 victims in his 'career' while the average boy molester studied offended 30.6 victims."[2]

The offender cannot stop offending unless he receives professional counseling. This is why it is vital that abused children be able to tell their parents what happened, and that their parents in turn notify the police.

Sexual abuse offenders seem to have these common characteristics:

> no close friends,
> feelings of inadequacy and low self-esteem,
> cannot distinguish between feelings and action, and so can't control their impulses.

Teenage Sexual Abuse Offenders

The majority of teenage sexual abuse offenders are boys. They seem to share these characteristics:

> no close friends,
> unable to relate to girls their own age,
> use sex as a way of releasing tension,
> poor, or no, relationship with father.

Please do not condemn all teenage boys, or cross them off your babysitter list. It is very important for young men to

---

[1] Information on these pages is adapted from Linda Tschirhart Sanford, *The Silent Children: A Parent's Guide to the Prevention of Child Sexual Abuse* (New York: McGraw-Hill Book Company), 1980, pp. 82-98.

[2] Ibid p. 85.

experience caring for young children. Here are some things you can do to make reasonably sure that your children are safe.

Before you hire any babysitter, male or female, get to know his or her family. Try to observe how family members interact with each other, how they talk with each other. Is each family member valued?

See if a babysitter's interest in being with small children is balanced by other interests involving friends of the same age. If not, you should be concerned.

Be aware if your child's relationship with the babysitter starts to become "exclusive" -- if time alone together becomes closely guarded.

Be sure to become acquainted with any older friends your child makes. Check out whether he has friends of his own age. Be wary if the relationship becomes exclusive.

Symptoms of Abuse and Stress
Some symptoms preschool children show when they are experiencing stress:

> sleep disturbances,
> eating disturbances,
> regressive behavior, for example, acting like a "baby,"

If they are experiencing sexual abuse they may also show:

> sudden fear of someone,
> sexual knowledge that you wouldn't expect them to have, such as knowledge of the "mechanics" of sex (ejaculation, intercourse, etc.)

Sexual Play
Sexual play among young children is very common, and represents no danger to healthy development.

However, if there is *any* coercion used - if a child is being held down, or unmercifully being teased for not participating - a parent should intervene.

If there is an age difference of five years or so between the children, sexual play is inappropriate and may indeed be abusive.

WHAT TO DO IF YOU SUSPECT ABUSE

1) *Go To A Private Place And Talk To Your Child.*

Many children believe they are still keeping the offender's secret even though their eating and/or sleeping patterns have changed, or their behavior has become noticeably regressive or different in some other way. If you observe these behavior changes and suspect your child has been sexually abused, ask him or her, "I'm wondering if someone has been touching you in a way you don't like or don't understand."

A child who has not been abused will probably react with surprise or disbelief that you could even think such a thing. If she has not been abused, but is behaving in a way which tells you something is wrong, asking if she has been abused may help her talk about what is really bothering her.

A child who has been abused may not admit it immediately. Remember she has been subjected to threats, bribes and extorted promises to keep the matter secret. Confronted by such a question, the abused child may retreat from you, look at the floor, cry or show other symptoms of nervousness. At this point you might say why you are asking: "I've noticed you've been spending a lot of time with _____, you've been having nightmares and you're not eating well. That's why I've been wondering..." If you remain gentle and calm, the child will begin to tell what happened, probably in a tentative, sketchy manner at first.

2) *Believe Your Child.*

Children do not lie about being abused. They cannot imagine, on their own, such a thing. In a private, quiet place *listen* to what your child has to say. Gently ask questions such as, "Has someone been touching you in a way that makes you feel bad?" and "Can you show me how he was touching you?" so that you fully understand what is going on.

14

As difficult as it may be, try to *remain calm*. You may feel outrage towards the offender, but a child would probably interpret this reaction as your being upset with her.

3) *Reassure Your Child.*

Tell her that she was right to have told you, that she has done nothing wrong, and that you will protect her from the offender.

Reassure her by talking with her, holding her, helping her get to sleep, whatever she needs - for as long as she needs it. If the child needs you to be with her for the rest of the day, stay with her.

4) *Call Child Protective Services (CPS) or the police.*

You must report the child's experience to either the police or CPS within 24 hours. Use your judgement as to when and how to call. Some children are vastly reassured by hearing their parents call to report; others are upset by this. In this second case, it will be best to wait until the child is otherwise occupied before you call CPS or the police. Either way, be sure to tell the child that a police officer, and a person from an agency which helps children, will be coming to hear her story.

5) *Offer Continuing Love And Support.*

The child may be burdened with guilt, feeling responsible for both the offense and all the difficulties attendant on her revealing what has happened. This feeling is magnified when the offender is a family member and the household is forceably separated as a result of her disclosure.

Most often, the prosecutor's case against the offender is based primarily on the victim's statement. It may seem to both you and your child that too many repetitions of the story are required, or that your child is questioned too closely. Your job during this time is to be by your child's side, offering your constant love and support. You may need to reassure your child quite often that this process is necessary to make sure she and other children are safe and that the offender gets the help he needs.

15

6) *Protect Your Child's Privacy.*

Siblings need to hear a brief, calm statement about what has happened. Other persons in the child's world - peers, teachers, relatives - can be told briefly and should also be asked to listen if the child wants to talk, but not to open any discussions themselves. Too many children who have experienced sexual abuse are treated as spectacles or as topics for gossip. Preserve the child's integrity as much as possible.

7) *Get Support For Yourself.*

Besides experiencing fear and outrage over what has happened, you may feel frightened about the consequences of the disclosure, especially if the offender is a close family member such as a father or brother. The child desperately needs your calm strength at this time. Use friends, relatives, professionals and 24-hour crisis lines to obtain the considerable emotional and possibly financial support you will need during this period. Don't try to bear this burden alone.

8) *Remember:*

The responsibility for the abuse lies solely with the offender. The fault is not yours or your child's.

CHAPTER 2
PREPARING PARENTS TO
DEAL WITH THIS SUBJECT

Parents are anxious to protect their children from sexual abuse, but they are frequently inhibited from doing so by not knowing how to begin, and by their own feelings of fear and helplessness concerning the whole subject.

This chapter is intended to help parents clarify their own understanding about what uncomfortable touch really is. The Touch Continuum and Personal Bubble activities are exercises to show how a person may feel pleased, or violated, by closeness depending on who is approaching and how she feels that day. They teach how our body signals when we are approached in any way which is uncomfortable to us. It is easier to help our children recognize these signals and act to protect themselves when we have identified these warning signals in ourselves.

Faced with an offender who is manipulating, exploiting or threatening, the child's *main defense* is making clear to the offender that he knows this is wrong, and that he will tell someone. In order to help our children describe what has happened to them in an abusive situation, we need to become acquainted with, and begin to use, anatomical words for sexual body parts. This section gives parents some hints on ways to make themselves more at ease with these words.

PERSONAL BUBBLE [1]

Purpose

Parents will become more aware of the idea of personal space.

How will this help prevent sexual abuse?

By discovering their own personal bubble, parents will be more aware of their children's personal bubbles, and will be more supportive of their children's choices about sharing their bodies.

Background

Another way to describe "uncomfortable feelings" is as *warning signals*. These are the physical reactions of our bodies to inappropriate touching situations, and while everyone's body can give warning signals, these signals are different for each one of us. The Personal Bubble game will help you learn about your body's warning signals.

Activities

★ Find a partner. Stand across the room from your partner. While you stand still, have your partner take very slow steps toward you. Look at each other's faces the whole time. As soon as you start to feel uncomfortable (when your warning signals start), tell your partner to stop. The distance left between you is your personal bubble of space. The warning signals you felt as your partner came too close were your body's way of protecting your bubble. What are your warning signals?

★ Repeat this game by playing it while kneeling to approximately the height of a child. Your partner should still stand up and walk. Remember to try and look at your partner's face as he/she moves toward you. Did your bubble size change?

★ Switch and give your partner a turn.

---

[1] The Personal Bubble activity is adapted from material developed by Caren Adams and Jennifer Fay. *No More Secrets* (San Luis Obispo, California: Impact Publishers) 1981. pp. 56-57.

TOUCH CONTINUUM [1]

Purpose

Parents can identify for themselves the kinds of touches which make them feel uncomfortable.

How will this help prevent sexual abuse?

Parents will be more aware of uncomfortable touch and will better understand the need to support their children's choices about touch.

Activity

★ Filling out a Touch Continuum can help you understand what "uncomfortable touch" means. Starting at the left side of the Continuum, write in the kinds of touch that feel good to you. Then fill in the kinds of touch that feel bad. Now write in touches that confuse you; touches that you aren't sure how to react to. An example might be a kiss from someone you don't know very well, or tickling that doesn't feel good anymore. After you've filled out the Continuum, take a moment to think about what you have written. Your preschooler's definitions of good, bad, and confusing touches would not be much different from yours. What is different, though, is that pre-schoolers don't always have the words to describe how they feel, and they are more unsure about how to react to confusing touches than are adults, even though their *feelings* are the same.

You can understand why it is so important for us to help our children learn to communicate their feelings about touch, and to support our children's choices about sharing their bodies with others.

---

[1] The Touch Continuum was developed by Cordelia Anderson Kent. See Personal Safety Curriculum: *Curriculum for Prevention of Child's Sexual Abuse.* Tacoma Public Schools, copyright 1981.

GOOD TOUCH	CONFUSING TOUCH	BAD TOUCH

If you'd like to complete the Touch Continuum with your pre-schoolers, you could use magazine pictures, or quickly draw pictures of the different kinds of touch as your child mentions them.

★ Start noticing in the next few days how and when your bubble size changes, depending on who you are with and what kind of situation you're in. Notice how, without thinking about it too much, people establish distance or closeness between themselves and others, and how quickly people react when their personal bubble is violated.

USING EYE CONTACT

Purpose

To give parents practice using eye contact as a way of improving communication and building self-esteem.

How will this help prevent sexual abuse?

Using eye contact when speaking and listening to children helps build self-esteem and therefore helps prevent sexual abuse. It will also help parents in coaching their children to say the phrases in *It's My Body* as though they really mean them.

Background

In the sections of this book titled "A Guided Reading of *It's My Body* with Your Child," we encourage parents to coach their children to say the phrases, "Don't touch me! I don't like it!" and "No, I won't touch you! I don't like it!" firmly and as though they mean them. One of the ways we can show that we really mean what we're saying is to maintain eye contact with the person we are talking to.

Eye contact *doesn't* mean staring. Maintaining eye contact means looking at the other person's face as you talk -- and as you listen -- to them. You can briefly look into the person's eyes and then glance away for a split second, or you may feel comfortable looking at the eyes for a longer period of time. You can even look at the nose or mouth, and the person will *think* you're looking into his or her eyes.

The benefits of eye-contact when you are *speaking* are:
- eye contact shows the other person you mean what you say;
- looking at the person's face (instead of the floor or out the window) shows the other person is a valuable part of the conversation and that you want to hear what is being said;
- eye contact implies to the other person that you are not nervous or ashamed about what you're saying; you are not afraid of him or her.

The benefits of eye contact when you are *listening* are:
- eye contact shows the other person you're interested in what is being said;

- looking the speaker in the face shows that you feel the other person is valuable and important;
- eye contact conveys to the other person that you're not nervous, afraid, or ashamed to hear what he or she has to say; you are not afraid of the speaker.

Activity

★ To experience the difference eye contact can make in a conversation, you can play this game with another adult:

1. Sit across from each other. Have your partner talk to you about anything for about half a minute. The whole time your partner is speaking, don't look at him or her. Look at the floor, or out the window, or at your lap.

2. Now, *you* talk, and your partner should not look at you the whole time you are talking.

Questions:
How did it feel to talk to someone when that person was not looking at you?

Did you try with your voice (making it louder), or with your body (moving closer to your partner) to get the other person to look at you?

How well could you listen to your partner when you weren't looking at him or her?

3. Repeat the exercise, but this time look at your partner's face and maintain eye contact when he or she is speaking. Then your partner should look at your face and maintain eye contact while you are speaking.

Questions:
Did it feel different to talk when the other person was looking at you?

How well did you listen when you were looking at the person while they were speaking?

Eye Contact With Children

Think about how small preschool children are. If you and your child are both standing, at what level are his or her eyes? (They are probably at your waist.) If your preschoolers want to have eye contact with you, they have got to crane their necks and look up very high. Yet, preschoolers gain the same benefits from eye contact as adults do.

You can help your children feel valuable and important by having as much eye contact with them as possible. Since they can't grow miraculously taller, this means that whenever possible you should bend down so that your face is level with theirs when you speak and when you listen to them.

You can see why it is important to coach your children to say the phrases in *It's MY Body* while looking an adult in the face. They are probably not used to looking at adult's faces (your neck gets tired if you have to look up all the time), and yet being able to do so can help them come across to the potential offender as if they mean "Don't touch me! I don't like it!"

GETTING COMFORTABLE WITH ANATOMICAL WORDS FOR BODY PARTS

Purpose

To give parents suggestions for how to be comfortable using anatomical words for body parts.

How will this help prevent sexual abuse?

Children and parents need to have the same vocabulary for body parts so that children can explain exactly what happened to them if they are sexually abused.

Background

One of the first steps in teaching children about sexual abuse is to make sure you have a common vocabulary for body parts. Having a common vocabulary for body parts is also very important in sexuality education. Anatomical words are penis, testicles, vagina, clitoris, breasts, etc.

Using these words instead of "cutesy" nicknames:
- shows respect for your child and his or her body.
- avoids association between the bathroom and sexuality. Nicknames like "pee pee" for the penis often have the effect of teaching a child that his or her sexual parts are "dirty."
- isn't funny or cute, and so can be used calmly and matter-of-factly.

Activities

Parents may have trouble using these anatomical words; they may feel embarrassed or uncomfortable. The activities below will help parents become more comfortable with this vocabulary.

★ Practice saying the anatomical words for the body's sexual parts. You can say "vagina, vagina, vagina" while you vacuum or use the chain saw and no one will hear you.

★ Practice saying the words in front of a mirror until you can say them comfortably and still look normal.

★ Start using the anatomical terms when talking with other adults.

★ You may never feel totally comfortable using these words, and that's okay. When you talk with your children, you can say something like, "Using these words is hard for me, but I'm going to do my best."

Here's Your Practice List:

Female Anatomy	*Male Anatomy*	*Human Anatomy*
Vagina	Penis	Anus
Clitoris	Testicles	Buttocks
Breasts/Nipples		Urethra
Vulva		

Resources

If your knowledge of anatomy is a little rusty, you can "brush up" by reading one of these books:

Family Book About Sexuality by Mary S. Calerone and Eric W. Johnson. An excellent book for learning about the body and for understanding how children and adults learn about sexuality.

Our Bodies Our Selves by The Boston Women's Health Book Collective. Written by women about women's bodies. This book is great not only for women to gain understanding about their bodies and themselves, but also for women to share with men.

Men's Bodies Men's Selves, by Sam Julty. Written for men as a guide to the health and well being of "body, mind and spirit." Also an excellent book for sharing with your partner.

CHAPTER 3
GUIDED READING OF "IT'S MY BODY" WITH YOUR CHILDREN

Children love to read *It's MY Body* over and over with their parents. After you and your children have become familiar with it, you may wish to use the following suggestions to help you "bring home its message."

The child in *It's MY Body* is meant to be male or female, so that you can refer to the child as "him" to your son or as "her" to your daughter. Preschoolers like to hear about children who are like themselves, and they will identify more easily with same-sex children.

Pages 1-4
Concept: Your body is uniquely your own. It is special and important just as it is.

Page 3 - Ask your children to guess what "it" is before you read page 4.

Page 4 - Ask your children to show you what their bodies are. You can explain that their bodies are from the tops of their heads to the soles of their feet. (Sometimes preschoolers think just one part is their "body" - they need to understand that the whole thing is their body.)

Ask your children to identify the parts of their bodies, including sexual parts. You may ask

> *"Where's your nose?"*
> *"Where's your penis?"*
> *"Where's your ankle?"*
> *"Where's your vagina?"*
> *"Where's your stomach?"*
>   etc.

Don't change your voice, or spend any more time on the sexual parts than on any of the others.

If your children don't know what you're talking about when you say "penis" or "vagina" - take some time in the next few days to identify their sexual parts for them.

You can say, "And your whole body belongs just to you."

Pages 5-9
Concept: Sometimes it feels good to share your body with others.

Personalize these pages for your children by asking questions like:

> "Who do you like to hug?"
> "Whose lap do you like to sit on?"
> "Who do you like to hold hands with?"

Who do *you* like to hold hands with, or hug? Tell your children about some of the times you like to share *your* body.

Page 9 - Ask your children:

> "Do you like to be tickled?"
> "Would you like to be tickled now?"

If they answer yes, tickle them gently, but stop *immediately* when they've had enough.

Page 10
Concept: Your body is always yours, even when you share it.

Ask your children:
> "How does the child in the picture feel?"
> "Can you hug your whole body?"
> "How do you feel today?"
> "What do you like about your body?"
> "When does your body make you happy?"

Pages 11-15
Concept: Sometimes it doesn't feel good to share your body.

Page 11 - Ask your children:

> "How does the child in the picture feel now?"
> "Can you make a face like that?"
> "How do you feel when you make that face?"

Personalize these pages by asking your children:

> "What's happening in this picture?"
> "When don't you like to share your body?"
> "Does this (being tickled too hard, held too tightly, etc.)
>   ever happen to you?"
> "How does that make you feel?"
> "How can you get them to stop?"

When does it feel uncomfortable for you to share *your* body?
Tell your children about some of these times.

Ask your children:

> "Do you ever tickle someone too hard?"
> "Why isn't it a good idea to do that?"

Pages 16-19
Concept: What to say and do if someone wants to share
         your body and you don't want to.

As you read the text on these pages, use lots of expression, and
read the phrases, "Don't touch me! I don't like it!" and "No, I
won't touch you! I don't like it!" in a way that models sternness
and assertiveness for your children.

Page 16 - Ask your children:

> "How does the child in the picture feel now?"
> "How can you tell the child feels like that?"

Page 16 - Comment on the way the illustrated child is standing.

29

Point out that the child's hand is up and that the child's face is stern.

Page 17 - Ask your children:

"How does the little girl in the picture feel when the other child says, 'Don't touch me! I don't like it!'?"

Ask your children:

"Are there times when you'd like to say 'Don't touch me, I don't like it!' or 'No, I won't touch you! I don't like it!' to someone?"

Pages 20-21

Concept: It's your children's turn to practice saying the phrases and taking the stances.

First have your children say the phrases with you, and then by themselves.

After practicing the phrases have them stand in front of you and say the phrases while taking the posture.

Coach your children to look you in the face, and not to giggle when they say the phrases.

When your children have said the phrases as though they really mean them, you can say, "You said that really well! I could tell you really meant it and you didn't sound afraid!"

Pages 22-24

Concept: Listening to your feelings about sharing your body.

Page 22 - Remind your children about the times they told you they liked to share their bodies. You can say, "Your body tells you by warm feelings that you like to share your body with your dad or a friend or me, etc."

Page 23 - Ask your children, "What can you say when you don't want to share your body?" and remind them of the phrase they just practiced.

Talk about some familiar situations when your children might use the phrases and postures taught in this book. For example, when another child grabs or pinches them, or an older brother or sister tickles too hard.

After you've finished reading *It's My Body*....

Give your children a hug. Tell them you read this book together because you love them. You can say to each child:

"I love you and I love your special body. We read this book so you can learn a way to take care of your body."

Tell your children that if anyone tries to share his or her body in a way that makes them uncomfortable, you want them to tell you about it, so you can make sure it doesn't happen again.

CHAPTER 4
WHAT CAN PARENTS DO TO MAKE CHILD SEXUAL ABUSE LESS LIKELY

Sexual abuse is far less likely when parents and teachers provide their children with tools for protecting themselves. This chapter suggests how people can interact in a manner which lets children know that they do not need to accept abuse from older people, and that they will be supported in not doing so.

A Touching Code can be agreed upon by the whole family to be used in any situation where another person's touch is uncomfortable. By including your children in the decision as to what the Touching Code will be, you demonstrate your respect for them. As the Touching Code becomes a part of your family's daily life, children will have many opportunities to practice making choices about touch, to develop awareness of other people's feelings; and to incorporate assertive communication into their relationships.

Children must feel good about themselves in order to refuse abuse from an older person. This chapter provides some practical ways you can show your children you value them by giving esteem-building messages, by fostering decision making and by helping your children become physically healthy.

Finally, since a child must tell someone if he is being abused, you must create a family environment in which feelings, and expressing them, are acceptable. This chapter provides ways to develop your children's "feeling" vocabulary and to show acceptance of feelings in your everyday lives.

THE TOUCHING CODE
WITH YOUR IMMEDIATE FAMILY

Purpose

Families can decide together on a Touching Code that all the family members can use.

How will this help prevent sexual abuse?

Having code words to say when they don't want to share their bodies gives children some control and power and, therefore, protects them.

Activity

★ Together, as a family, decide upon a code word or phrase that everyone in the family can use when they don't want to be touched. It might simply be "No" or "Please don't," or you may wish to use the phrases in *It's MY Body*: "Don't touch me! I don't like it!" and "No, I won't touch you! I don't like it!"

After your family has decided upon the Touching Code, make sure all family members understand their right to use the code and that they respect the use of the code by all family members.

★ Our family's Touching Code is:

_____

_____

POINTS TO PONDER

Everyone has the right to decide what kinds of touch feel good and what kinds of touch don't feel good.

If your child or partner doesn't want to be touched "right now," it doesn't mean they don't love you.

The Touching Code never needs to be followed by excuses or explanations.

TOUCHING CODE
AMONG RELATIVES

Purpose

To help parents think of ways to explain the Touching Code to relatives.

How will this help prevent sexual abuse?

Children will only believe and use the Touching Code if they see that there are no exceptions to the code.

Background

Touching situations with relatives might seem harder to deal with than those involving strangers or friends. But in order for the Touching Code to work as a protective strategy, children must be sure that there are no exceptions. That is, even relatives who love them and who they love don't have the right to force children to share their bodies when they don't want to. Children will be more likely to use the code in a potentially abusive situation if they've been supported for using it in "safe" situations.

Activities

To make it easier for you to support your children's choices about sharing their bodies with relatives, you can:

★ Explain to relatives that you've been talking about touching with your children as a way of protecting them from sexual abuse, and that it's important for children to be able to practice saying "No!" to grownups when they don't want to be touched.

★ You can share *It's My Body* with relatives and talk about the things you and your children have learned about touch.

★ Most importantly, you and your children can decide upon some alternatives that they can use instead of sharing their bodies.

    For example:

        shaking hands,
        blowing a kiss,
        coloring a picture to say "thank you."

35

THE TOUCHING CODE
AMONG OTHERS

Purpose

To support children's right to choose not to share their bodies, parents need to be able to explain the Touching Code to others.

How will this help prevent sexual abuse?

The more children practice the code and are supported for doing so, the more likely they will be to use it in a potentially abusive situation; and the more unlikely it is that they will keep the situation a secret.

Background

Notice how often children are expected to share their bodies when they don't want to, not just with family members, but with people they don't even know. For example, adults may pick up small children in the grocery store, or automatically pat children's heads. Always support your children's wishes at these times. *You* would not want to hug a stranger in the grocery store, nor would you pinch an adult's cheek or pat their heads without thinking. Respect your children's wishes to resist uncomfortable touches.

Activity

★ Role play supporting your child's choice. Pretend you are in a store and someone strokes your child. You might say:

"In our family, we say 'No' when we don't want to be touched. It's called our Touching Code. I think Bobby is trying to use our Touching Code right now. Please don't hug him when he doesn't want to be hugged."

What are some other touching alternatives you and your children can think of?

_____

_____

_____

POINT TO PONDER

Forcing children to share their bodies when they don't want to teaches them you care more for the feelings of others than you care for them.

SHARING ONE'S BODY WITH A DOCTOR

When your children visit the doctor or dentist, they need to share their bodies whether they want to or not. We believe the best way to handle these situations is to approach them honestly and positively. You can explain to your children that sometimes their bodies need special care that only a doctor or dentist knows how to give and because their bodies are neat and special, you want to be sure they are taken care of. Be honest, tell your children calmly that the shot will hurt or the novacaine will feel funny but that it's necessary and will be over soon. Please don't tell your children that the *doctor* or *dentist* will hurt them. Make it clear that it's the shot or the novacaine, etc., that hurts. You might say: "This will hurt for a short time so your body can feel good for a long time." Make sure your doctor or dentist will allow you to be with your child during the visit.

DEVELOP POSITIVE SELF-IMAGE:
GIVE ESTEEM—BUILDING MESSAGES [1]

Purpose

To practice giving children messages that will build their self-esteem.

How will this help prevent sexual abuse?

Children who have positive self-esteem will not need to develop a "secret" relationship with an adult to feel good about themselves.

Background

Children receive many messages about who they are and how well they are doing. Messages about how you value them are called *being* messages. These are unconditional and unearned. Messages about how well they are doing are *doing* messages. They are earned and conditional, dependent upon performance.

Some of these messages are positive and some are negative. Positive being and doing messages encourage self-esteem. They help a child feel lovable and capable. Negative being and doing messages decrease a child's self-esteem.

Examples of positive being messages are: I love you, I'm glad you're my boy/girl, I like to be near you, Your needs are important to me.

Examples of positive doing messages are: Good thinking, You put away your toys well, I enjoy watching you dance, and You set the table before I asked. Thank you.

Examples of negative being messages: Get lost, What, You again, and I wish I weren't a parent.

Examples of negative doing messages: Not another accident! Can't you ever do anything right, and You left your toys out as usual. (Some negative doing messages can be positive if the idea is that, although you made a mistake this time, you are really capable. For example, You know better than to walk on the flowers. Next time look where you are going.)

[1] copyright © Elizabeth Crary 1984

Activities

★ Give being messages directly. Write three being messages for each child. They can be verbal, like the above suggestions, or non-verbal, like a hug. Decide when you could give them.

first child

(1) _____

(2) _____

(3) _____

second child

(1) _____

(2) _____

(3) _____

★ Make up a non-verbal being message. This could be a sign or signal that says "I love you." For example, one Mom gives three little squeezes for "I love you." She can use it when she is on the phone, in church or other times when she doesn't want to speak.

My non-verbal being sign is: _____

_____

★ Give doing messages directly. To prepare, write three doing messages for each child. Decide when you could give them.

first child

(1) _____

(2) _____

(3) _____

second child

(1) _____

(2) _____

(3) _____

★ Give messages indirectly. Some children like to over-hear a parent saying nice things about them to another parent or friend. At other times children like to hear a report that someone else said something nice. (For example, Mom says, "Dad told me he really appreciated that you brought in the trash containers.")

★ Make up a non-verbal doing message. You can use the "okay" sign, thumbs up sign or make up your own signal that means "You did a good job." Again it can be used in situations where you are not near enough to speak or for some reason don't want to. It would be especially useful for encouraging children to use the Touching Code.

My non-verbal "good for you" sign is: _____

_____

DEVELOP POSITIVE SELF-IMAGE:
BUILDING A HEALTHY BODY IMAGE

Purpose

To give parents some ideas for developing a good body image in their children.

How will this help prevent sexual abuse

The more a child values something, the more care she/he will take in sharing it.

Background

Each one of us has a mental and emotional "picture" of our body, and we respect and enjoy our bodies to differing degrees. Preschoolers are generally much more "at home" in their bodies than are most adults, having not yet fully absorbed the ideas that "all girls should be thin" or "all boys must be strong." We can take advantage of this natural enjoyment small children have in their bodies by continuing to nurture our children's joy and respect for their bodies now and as they grow older.

Activities

★ Allow your children plenty of opportunity for dancing, running, climbing, jumping, skipping.

★ Model positive body images yourself.

★ Remember back to the games you played as a child: freeze, tag, baby in the air, kickball, Chinese jump rope, even TV tag and flashlight tag. Your children may love to play, so teach them or play with them.

★ Dance with your children. One of the great things about children is that they are not sophisticated and experienced dancers; they won't laugh at you.

★ Talk about television role models. Our society tends to promote fairly rigid ideals concerning shape, size, and strength of human bodies. Television advertisements in particular relay the message that we are beautiful and worthy in direct proportion to how we measure up to those rigid ideals. The fear that we don't measure up is often a motivation to begin sexual relationships. Teenagers are especially susceptible to this kind of pressure, and may view sexual relationships as a way of proving their attractiveness.

★ One way to foster feelings of worth in children regardless of their shape, size or appearance is to stop using these as a basis for compliments or praise. Rather, begin focusing on the particular qualities you enjoy in your children: sense of humor, ability to make friends and enthusiasm. This will teach your children to value all their qualities, rather than just their physical appearance. You might say: "I noticed how well you get along with your friends," or, "I love it when you make me laugh." Find other things to say about people besides that they are pretty or fat.

TALK ABOUT FEELINGS:
DEVELOP A FEELING VOCABULARY

Purpose
To help children learn to identify their feelings by providing them with descriptive words.

How will this help prevent sexual abuse?
Being able to recognize feelings which are warning signals helps children recognize and resist uncomfortable touch.

Background
Part of learning to trust and accept one's feelings is being able to identify them. Feelings are warning signals which help children recognize and resist uncomfortable touch. By learning the words to describe feelings, children can better identify them.

Often, we ourselves cannot explain how we feel about an incident or person because our thoughts are confused and maybe even conflicting. Abused children are frequently in this same situation, especially since the majority are abused by people they know and care about. Not surprisingly then, their feelings of fear, anger and guilt may be mixed with love for and a desire to please and protect the offender.

Talking with children about feelings as a part of your day to day life will more fully prepare them to recognize the discomfort, guilt and confusion which arises in someone who has been abused. Giving children words for describing how they feel makes this easier.

The easiest time to begin is with toddlers and preschoolers whose avid explorations include learning about feelings. Very young children need to be able to "check out" their usually intense emotions with adults.

Activity
★ The following chart lists some suggested "feeling" words. You may use the list to help spark your memory of specific situations where you had that feeling, and then try to describe them verbally. Begin to use some of these words in

conversations about feelings with your children. You might also share your deep feelings with your children by telling them stories based on the situations you have described in your chart.

Comfortable	Uncomfortable
excited	lonely
secure	dejected
loved	cranky
proud	hurt
challenged	insecure
competent	frustrated
happy	jealous
calm	nervous

ACCEPT AND EXPRESS FEELINGS
IN DAILY LIFE

Purpose

To help your family develop an environment in which all feelings are acceptable.

How will this help prevent sexual abuse?

Children must have learned to respect what their feelings are telling them if they are to be able to resist or report uncomfortable touch.

Activities

The following are suggested ways of showing your acceptance of your children's feelings.

★ Avoid labeling feelings as "good" or "bad." Your children may interpret these labels as describing them rather than their emotion. Feelings themselves are neither good nor bad, they just are. They should not be confused with behaviors, which can be good or bad.

★ Legitimize your children's feelings. When we tell our children "Oh, that's nothing to be afraid of" or "You shouldn't feel angry about a little thing like that," we shut the door on our children's willingness to tell us how they feel. We also convey the message that children's feelings are not legitimate or real.

★ Help children connect and verbalize feelings about touch by using comments such as, "I feel happy when you give me surprise hugs," "I feel so relaxed when you brush my hair" or "I feel angry when I'm pinched like that."

★ Every so often ask open-ended questions such as "How would you feel if your friend asked you to do something you didn't want to do?" or "How would you feel if your block tower got knocked down by accident/on purpose?"

Questions like these offer parents an opportunity to talk about feelings with their children and may open up pathways for problem-solving or empathy such as: "I know you felt afraid to tell Johnny you couldn't play with him so let's try to think about what you could say to him next time," or "How do you think Sally feels when you knock her blocks down?"

★ Enjoy and encourage spontaneous affection from your children. Be sure to reinforce your children for expressing affection, boys as well as girls. Boys who have not been discouraged from expressing affection will be better able to resist our society's teaching that males should be affectionate only in a sexual way, and only towards females. This idea is damaging to males, and endangers females. Teenage boys who cannot express their need for nonsexual affection (just being hugged, holding a baby, etc.) often resort to sexual intercourse as the only way to fulfill those needs. Do not limit your sons' growth by denying them shared, nonsexual affection.

★ Share your uncomfortable as well as comfortable feelings with your children, but be careful not to expect them to accept responsibility for how you feel. Yelling at your kids because your boss yelled at you makes your children responsible for your feelings. Instead, look for other ways to help yourself feel better.

PLAY FEELING GAMES AND ACTIVITIES

Purpose

To help parents and children identify and talk about feelings.

How will this help prevent sexual abuse?

These activities will also help parents and children accept their feelings. Children will learn that their feelings are real and legitimate and that their parents will not "turn off" when they need to talk about or express their feelings. It helps prevent the "secret" of sexual abuse.

Activities

★ Collect pictures and make up stories about what's happening in the pictures with your children, specifically focusing on feelings.

★ Glue pictures onto the sides of a small box and devise a tossing game. Toss the box to your children and ask them to make up a story about the people in the picture that is facing them as they catch the box. Your children can then toss the box back and you can make up a story.

★ To help your children begin to recognize and talk about their feelings, you can make a "feelings chart" together to hang on their bedroom door, or in some other prominent place.

First assemble the materials listed below and have your children help you make the chart. You will need:

one square of poster board, 12" x 12" or larger;
four circles cut out of poster board;
four envelopes;
four paper clips;
glue;
hole punch;
scissors;
markers or crayons.

To Make:

1. Draw faces representing feelings on four circles.

happy   calm   mad   afraid

Other emotions might include: silly, content, luxuriating, nurtured, loving/loved, angry, shy, lonely, jealous, hurt, sorry.

2. Draw the same faces on the envelopes.
3. Glue the envelopes across the bottom of the poster board square.
4. Punch a hole in the top of each circle face, and put a bent paper clip through each hole, so that the clip makes a hook.
5. Write your child's name at the top of the square.
6. Underneath your child's name, write:
> How I feel
7. Punch a small hole underneath the words:
> How I feel
8. Put the circle faces into the four envelopes--the happy face in the happy envelope, and mad face in the mad envelope, etc.

9. Your feeling chart should look like this:

Explain to your children that they can choose one of the feeling faces that shows how they feel at that time and hang it up on the chart (by slipping the bent paper clip through the hole.)

49

Pick a special time of the day when your children can hang up their feeling face. You may wish to choose bedtime, and use the feeling face as a summary of the whole day. Or, you may wish to choose after breakfast, especially if there is a special event, or not-so-special event, happening that day that you think your children have strong feelings about.

Be sure to tell your children that they can change their face during the day if their feelings change.

Set aside time to listen to your children talk about why they chose the face they did.

★ Variations on the "Feeling Chart":

1. Have your children make up words and faces for their own feelings.

2. Use pieces of colored fabric to hang up instead of the faces, with various colors corresponding to various emotions.

3. Have your children make sounds with their mouths, fists, etc., to express their emotions.

ENCOURAGE DECISION-MAKING: GIVE CHILDREN CHOICES

Purpose

To remind parents that even very small children can, and should, have the opportunity to make choices.

How will this help prevent sexual abuse?

It's MY Body is based on the idea that kids can choose when, how, and by whom they want to be touched. The more practice a child has making choices, the more confident he or she will be about making them.

Background

One important part of self-esteem is feeling that you have choices about the things you do, and have control over your life.

Preschoolers are just finding out about choices and control and, realistically, don't have a whole lot of either. *It's MY Body* teaches that children can make choices about sharing their bodies, and that they have some means to control with whom, when, and how to share their bodies. It's important that you reinforce this teaching by giving your preschoolers as much choice and control as possible. This way, your children are sure to practice making decisions, and also to learn that what they think and feel matters to you.

Activities

★ On a cold day, your child must wear a coat, but he may choose his red one or his blue one.

★ A child may not play with Dad's tools, but she can cut with her own scissors, or "paint" on a wall with water.

A good formula for explaining choices to preschoolers is:

No, you may not _____ , because _____ .
But you may _____ or _____ .
You must _____ , because _____ , and
you can choose _____ or _____ .

★ Decide what choice your children could have in these situations.

1. Time to go to bed.

_____ or _____

2. The child wants to run away from you rather than walk beside you.

_____ or _____

3. The child wants to pull the kitten's tail.

_____ or _____

(possible answers)
1. You may wear blue pajamas or red pajamas.
2. You may walk beside me or I will carry you.
3. You may pet the kitty gently or pull on a rope.

Remember: All alternatives must be okay with you.

ENCOURAGE DECISION MAKING:
PLAY "WHAT WOULD YOU DO IF...?"[1]

Purpose
To give children practice thinking of ways they could deal with difficult or uncertain situations.

How will this help prevent sexual abuse?
Children who have had practice thinking of "what to do" in fun situations will be more able to think of "what to do" in abusive situations.

Background
Most children find it difficult to think creatively in a crisis situation. However they can recall information learned or figured out beforehand. The more recent the information was refreshed, the more easily it can be recalled under stress. Try reviewing many kinds of situations, both silly and serious.

Activities

★ Tell your children stories about experiences (both funny and serious) that happened to you as a child. Include feelings and the factors you considered as well as what you did. If you have learned a better way to handle the situation since then, discuss that too.

★ Play "What Would You Do If...?" Describe a situation and ask your child "What would you do if...?" Some suggestions are listed below. Make up situations that reflect the problems your child might face.

1. You left your lunch money at home.
2. You are at camp. A friend wants you to take a picture of someone who is dressing.
3. Your mother is lying on the floor. She doesn't answer when you talk to her.
4. A big child lifts up your dress to see what you are wearing underneath.
5. You left your coat on the school bus.

---

[1] copyright © Elizabeth Crary 1984

6. A grown-up asks to see your vagina (or penis).
7. Someone is tickling you and you want them to stop.
8. Someone tells you they will give you something you really like (for example, ice cream cone, doll) if you do something secret.
9. You and your parents went to the store. You got lost.

10. A grownup you don't like wants to hug you.

REMEMBER: Thinking of ideas is more important than "remembering" what they were told.

ENCOURAGE DECISION MAKING: MAKE IT EASIER FOR A CHILD TO TELL

Purpose

To make it easier for the child to tell on someone bigger and more powerful than she is.

How will this help prevent sexual abuse?

If a child's reports about others have been listened to in day-to-day situations, she will be more able to tell someone about the abuse in spite of the offender's powerful pressure not to.

Background

A "rule of thumb" is that children need to have three or four trusted adults, besides their parents, whom they feel they could tell if they are sexually abused. Having words and knowing who to tell is not always enough; children need to believe they will be listened to.

One of the things the offender counts on is the child's silence; as long as the child does not tell anyone about the abuse, the offender is generally safe. Therefore the offender goes to great lengths to ensure the child's silence. Threats, the enticement of having a secret, bribes, and a general air that the abuse is perfectly okay and is really only a way of expressing love for the child, are all used by the offender to enlist the child's cooperative silence. Furthermore, since children are usually chastized for "telling on" other children, they feel pressure not to tattle on an adult.

Children will know it's okay to tell if parents have discussed sexual abuse with them, and have demonstrated trust in their feelings, reactions and perceptions. Here are some additional ways we can help children feel confident about telling the offender's secret.

Activities

★ Playing "Who would you tell" is one way of generating a "list" of resource people for children.

> "Who would you tell besides me if someone touched you in an uncomfortable way?"

"My teacher."

"Who would you tell if she didn't believe you?"

"Sally, next door."

"Who would you tell if she didn't believe you?"...and so
on.

Like many of us, children can say difficult things more easily
if they just have a way to begin.

★ Giving children a sentence to say if they need to tell you about
being abused is helpful. This can simply be, "If you ever have
to use your Touching Code with an older person, you need to
tell me. You can say, 'I had to use my Touching Code with
(my babysitter, my friend Joe, Uncle George) today.' When
you say that I'll know just what you're trying to tell me and
then we can talk about it."

★ Differentiate types of secrets. Secrets can be differentiated
from surprises in that secrets are never supposed to be told,
whereas surprises are always eventually disclosed. Since
secrets can be dangerous, give your children some rules to
help them determine which ones should be revealed.

1) We do not keep secrets when that would hurt someone.
2) Adults or older people should never ask children to keep
   secrets from their parents.

Though very young children will have difficulty understanding these concepts, literal explanations of the above,
with plenty of examples, are appropriate beginning at about
age six. Meanwhile, in your day to day life with preschoolers,
begin describing birthday presents and special events as
surprises rather than secrets.

★ Listen to your children when they "tattle." What you need to
do when children "tell on" someone is to listen, and to suggest
ways they can deal with the problem. For example, if your
child runs to you to tell you that Joey "said a bad word," you
can say something like, "You need to tell Joey you don't like
to hear that word."

Intervene when necessary but try to structure your interventions around what the child can do to solve the problem.

Children are more likely to tell the offender's secret if their "tattling" has been taken seriously and listened to. Show them that children can be helped and supported in solving their problems.

★ Finally emphasize over and over in your words and actions that your children can talk to you about anything. To best protect your children from sexual abuse, you need to provide them with an atmosphere of acceptance, openness, and respect.

CONCLUSION

Child sexual abuse can be prevented. This book has been written in order to give encouragement and practical suggestions to adults committed to preventing this crime. The nature of sexual abuse--which involves betrayal of trust, manipulation and misuse of power--makes it an issue of essential importance for families and schools.

The activities and information in this book have shown that preventive teaching need not be terrifying to children or sensationalistic. Indeed, the preventive strategies suggested here are founded upon some very positive concepts concerning child development and well being. Support of a child's growing sense of mastery, modeling and teaching assertiveness (which is a form of communication based on one's *feelings*), and recognizing a child's right to decide how, when and by whom she or he wishes to be touched, are prevention strategies which in and of themselves promote a child's well being.

We hope that this book and the accompanying children's book, *It's MY Body*, provide you and your children with many opportunities to show thoughts, ideas and feelings with each other; for it is truly this kind of sharing between adults and children which acts to prevent sexual abuse.

APPENDIX

Where to go for more information

BOOKS FOR PARENTS

No More Secrets by Caren Adams and Jennifer Fay, Impact Publishers, 1981.

This is an excellent book for parents on sexual abuse. It provides language suggestions and information on what to do if your child is sexually abused.

Self-Esteem: A Family Affair by Jean Illsley Clark, Winston Press, Inc., 1978.

Your Child's Self-Esteem by Dorothy Corkville Briggs, Doubleday & Company, Inc., 1970.

Both of these books are excellent resources for parents wanting to know more about the development of high self-esteem in children. *Your Child's Self-Esteem* gives background information and good, practical ideas. *Self-Esteem: A Family Affair* includes worksheets, parenting tips, and case histories. Both are highly recommended.

BOOK FOR CHILDREN

No More Secrets For Me by Oralle Watcher, Little Brown & Co., 1983,

This book contains four short stories about children who are experiencing uncomfortable touching. The children do tell someone else and are listened to. Not scary or lurid, this book is excellent for elementary age children.

OTHER RESOURCES FOR PARENTS AND CHILDREN

In many cities organizations have been formed to teach children how to say "no" to uncomfortable touch. These use puppets, stories and pictures to emphasize to the children not to keep the offender's secret. In other cities, applied theater groups present plays about touching, saying "no" and telling someone. Some of the places to check for information about such groups in your area are:

> treatment centers for child abuse victims
> 24-hour crisis lines

school counseling offices

sexual assault centers

School districts around the country have begun implementing "personal safety" curriculums which teach children the skills of assertiveness, recognizing potentially dangerous situations, defining sexually abusive touch, and who and how to tell if they are abused. The content of these curriculums should be available for review by parents. You may wish to consult with your child's teacher so that you can reinforce these teachings at home.

Children's Protective Services, treatment centers and sexual assault centers often have speakers available for parent groups.

PARENTING PRESS, INC.

Presents
Additional books for kids, parents and people who work with them.

IT'S MY BODY
by Lory Freeman

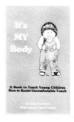

This children's book can be used alone or in conjunction with *A Parents' Resource Guide*. It offers children a strategy for dealing with uncomfortable touch whether it is tickling or more serious abuse.

24 pages, 5½ x 8½   *$3.50 paperback*

KIDS CAN COOPERATE
by Elizabeth Crary

Kids **can** cooperate IF they have the skills. Elizabeth Crary describes how to teach children the skills they need to solve conflicts themselves.

102 pages, 8½ x 11   *$8.95 paperback*

WITHOUT SPANKING OR SPOILING

A PRACTICAL APPROACH TO TODDLER AND PRESCHOOL GUIDANCE
by Elizabeth Crary

This book includes lots of ideas to reduce child-parent conflicts without resorting to physical violence. It is easy to understand, easy to use and appropriate for use with young children.

102 pages, 8½ x 11   *$8.95 paperback*

THE TROUBLE WITH SECRETS
by Karen Johnsen

"Your child's best friend wants to know where she keeps your house key." "An older schoolmate takes your child's lunch and tells him not to tell" This book helps children distinguish between secrets that may hurt or worry people and surprises that do not.

5½ x 8½. 32 pages, $3.95 paper

LOVING TOUCHES
by Lory Freeman

Loving Touches is a warm, gentle book for young children about positive, caring touch. It presents the idea that "loving touches" are necessary to healthy living and shows children how to ask for them.

5½ x 8½, 32 pages, $3.50 paper

≡ ORDER FORM ≡

PLEASE SEND THE FOLLOWING BOOKS:

IT'S MY BODY	$3.50	————
LOVING TOUCHES	$3.50	————
KIDS CAN COOPERATE	$8.95	————
WITHOUT SPANKING OR SPOILING	$8.95	————
THE TROUBLE WITH SECRETS	$3.95	————

NAME _____   SUBTOTAL _____

ADDRESS _____   SHIPPING _____

CITY _____   SALES TAX _____
                              (Wash. State 7.9%)

STATE _____ ZIP _____   TOTAL _____

VOLUME DISCOUNTS AVAILABLE - write for information

Send check or Money Order to:
    Parenting Press, Inc.
    7744 - 31st Ave. NE
    Suite 408
    Seattle, WA 98115

Order Subtotal	Shipping
$ 0-$10	add $1 25
$10-$25	add 2 25
$25-$50	add 3 25

Prices Subject To Change